Warning: Small parts may be a choking hazard. Not for children under 3 years.

ACKNOWLEDGEMENTS

Editorial Director: Erin Conley

Designers: Jeanette Miller, Lynn Gustafson, Lisa Yordy

Special thanks to Jenny Brennan, Suzanne Cracraft, Emily Jocson, Jennifer Ko, Cris Lehman, Maria Llull, Lani Stackel, Tami Sartor and Rosie Slattery for their invaluable assistance!

Many thanks to all of the terrific kids who contributed questions to this game:
Mrs. Mrozowski's 5th grade class at Ryan Elementary School, Mrs. Birkbeck's 4th grade class,
Ms. Barnett's 4th grade class and Ms. Poper's 5th grade class at Ford Elementary School,
Maxwell Brown, Melissa Brown, Jake Burkhead, Dillon Cox, Kaitlin D'Allocco, Simon Ehrlich,
Mario Gutierrez, Ashley Hebert, Kyle Obst, Olivia Patsos, Alaina Patsos, Emma Roos,
Jake Schlackman, Arianna Smith, Marissa Smith, Caroline Williams, Lauren Williams,
Tommy Williams and Tanisha Wills.

ISBN 1-57528-921-0

Printed in China.

CONTENTS

Introduction

Just as every picture tells a story, I find that every book I write has a story. *Kids Battle the Grown-Ups* got its start at a very special private elementary school called The San Francisco School in San Francisco, CA. I volunteered to teach an elective there on board game production and development. The course ran for eight weeks and the object of it was to create a marketable game. The class consisted of six very enthusiastic and interested 12 year olds. Actually, two of the kids, Jake and Mario, weren't that enthusiastic but they still did a great job.

The kids and I worked together to identify themes and game play that would be interesting to middle school students and their parents. The kids used their math, art and research skills to assist in the development of the game board, the game play and the game content/questions. My hope was that we could publish the game and share some of the proceeds with the school. I never imagined the success we would have.

Two years later we are still selling the game, which has been translated into German, French and Dutch. It has also been nominated for Game of the Year in the Netherlands. This book is a great new version, inviting you and your parents (or kids) to see how much fun can be had when kids try to show grown-ups who knows more.

My creative team of Hannah Roos, Jake Burkhead, Mario Gutierrez, Dillon Cox, Simon Ehrlich, Jake Schlackman and Tanisha Wills join me in wishing you hours of fun playing and reading *Kids Battle the Grown-Ups*.

—Bob

RULES

Object

To be the first team to earn 15 points—and find out who knows more:
kids or grown-ups!

Playing the Game

1. First things first: grab a pen and paper to keep track of your points.

2. Divide players into two teams: kids vs. grown-ups.

3. The kids spin first to determine which team will get to answer a set of questions.
    A set consists of three questions (in other words, all the questions on the page!).

4. *If the spinner lands on the **kid's only** zone*, a player from the grown-up's team
    reads the kids the first set of questions from the kid's question section.

5. *If the spinner lands on the **grown-up's only** zone*, a player from the kid's team
    reads the grown-ups the first set of questions from the grown-up's question section.

6. *If the spinner lands on the **both teams** zone*, a player from the grown-up's
    team reads the kids a set of questions from the kid's question section. Then a player
    from the kid's team reads the grown-ups a set of questions from the grown-up's
    question section.

7. *Teams earn one point for each question answered correctly.* (For example, if the kids answer 2 questions right, they get 2 points. The maximum a team may earn in a given round is 3 points. Got it? Good!)

8. Play now continues and the grown-ups take a spin.

Winning the Game

The first team to earn 15 points wins the game!

Questions
for
Kids

Q: Which continent is home to Mount Kilimanjaro?

A: Africa

Q: What store hosts a Thanksgiving Day parade in New York City every year?

A: Macy's

Q: Which of these plays was not written by Shakespeare: *The Odd Couple*, *Romeo and Juliet* or *Othello*?

A: *The Odd Couple*

Q: What TV show debuted in 1978 and starred Robin Williams?

A: *Mork and Mindy*

Q: Coretta Scott married what civil rights leader and ordained minister?

A: Dr. Martin Luther King, Jr.

Q: Who is the President of the US Senate: the President, the Vice President or the Speaker of the House?

A: The Vice President

7

Q: Was Franklin D. Roosevelt a Republican or a Democrat?

A: Democrat

8

Q: In what country would you find the town of Cheddar?

A: England

9

Q: What animal did Elvis Presley sing was "cryin' all the time"?

A: A hound dog

Q: Put these Disney movies in chronological order, by date of release: *Mulan*, *Pinocchio* and *Cinderella*.

A: *Pinocchio*, *Cinderella* and *Mulan*

Q: What reference book is Roget famous for?

A: The thesaurus

Q: Is Frank Lloyd Wright famous for his buildings, his books or his bowling balls?

A: His buildings

13

Q: What is the name of Madonna's first album: *Madonna*, *Like a Prayer* or *Music*?

A: *Madonna*

14

Q: What is a tilde: a language symbol, a tractor or a kind of underpants?

A: A language symbol (used in español, among others)

15

Q: Name two states that border the Gulf of Mexico.

A: Texas, Louisiana, Alabama, Florida, Mississippi

 Q: Is basil an animal, vegetable or mineral?

A: Vegetable

 Q: What do we call the depressing era of poverty the United States experienced in the 1930s?

A: The Great Depression

 Q: On what 1970s TV show did Redd Foxx play a junk dealer with a son named Lamont?

A: *Sanford and Son*

 19

Q: Who was Jerry Lewis' comedy partner?

A: Dean Martin

 20

Q: Which scientific discipline's name means "the study of life": chemistry, biology or physics?

A: Biology

 21

Q: In which of the 50 states would you find The Grand Canyon?

A: Arizona

Q: How many kids are in the Brady Bunch?

A: 6

Q: The last US state, alphabetically, also has the lowest population. What is it?

A: Wyoming

Q: What two common household ingredients can you put together to make paste?

A: Flour and water

Q: Is Madagascar an African island, an art museum or a raceway?

A: An African island

Q: Who is Sherlock Holmes' trusty aide?

A: Dr. Watson

Q: Would you be more likely to have tiramisu before dinner, during dinner or after dinner?

A: After dinner (It's an Italian dessert!)

28

Q: If you are Dutch, where were you most likely born: the Netherlands, Belgium or Germany?

A: The Netherlands (also called Holland)

29

Q: Which Spanish painter had a famous "blue" period?

A: Pablo Picasso

30

Q: What kind of animal is a Jack Russell terrier?

A: A dog

 Q: Danes are natives of what country?

A: Denmark

 Q: What country had Pierre Trudeau as its Prime Minister: Canada, France or Algeria?

A: Canada

 Q: Who wrote *A Tale of Two Cities* and *A Christmas Carol*?

A: Charles Dickens

Q: Name at least two of the four Beatles.

A: Paul, John, George, Ringo

Q: Who has been chairman of the Federal Reserve since 1987?

A: Alan Greenspan

Q: What country was home to Gandhi: India, Korea or Spain?

A: India

 Q: Would pungent describe a smell or a shell?

A: A smell

 Q: When a couple takes a trip just after their wedding, what is that vacation called?

A: A honeymoon

 Q: What holiday did Bob Hope celebrate with TV specials for many years?

A: Christmas

Q: How many kittens would a mother cat be more likely to give birth to in one litter: 1, 6 or 16?

A: 6

Q: What movie musical features dancing battles between gangs called the Jets and the Sharks?

A: *West Side Story*

Q: What city hosts the Miss America pageant?

A: Atlantic City

43

Q: What Louisiana city is known as "The Big Easy"?

A: New Orleans

44

Q: Elton John and Liberace are both famous for their outrageous costumes, but they also play(ed) the same musical instrument. What is it?

A: The piano

45

Q: What is 30% of 100?

A: 30

Q: What is the name of Bill Gates' corporation?

A: Microsoft®

Q: Name the TV show that featured Bo and Luke Duke racing around in a car called the General Lee.

A: *The Dukes of Hazzard*

Q: What did American colonists send to the King of England to declare independence from his country?

A: The Declaration of Independence

Q: Which came first: *The Simpsons* or *The Flintstones*?

A: *The Flintstones*

Q: Name one of the two countries that share the longest undefended border in the world.

A: Canada, the United States

Q: Is Jack Nicklaus a famous gardener, golfer or gourmet chef?

A: Golfer

Q: Academy Awards and a famous grouch share the same name. What is it?

A: Oscar

Q: What vehicles were featured in the movie *Easy Rider*: motorcycles, helicopters or submarines?

A: Motorcycles

Q: Which state's name is Spanish for "mountain"?

A: Montana

Q: Is Andy Warhol famous for pies, pictures or perfumes?

A: Pictures

Q: When a Latina girl has a special quinceañera birthday party, how old is she?

A: 15

Q: Was MTV born in the '70s, the '80s or the '90s?

A: The '80s

 Q: What is the name of John Lennon's second wife?

A: Yoko Ono

 Q: What is Vidal Sassoon famous for: cutting hair, making chairs or teddy bears?

A: Cutting hair

 Q: If you're a girl doing the tango, what might you be holding in your teeth?

A: A rose

 61

Q: Would you be more likely to find a dangling participle in an essay or on a construction site?

A: In an essay

 62

Q: What clothing company makes Dockers®?

A: Levi Strauss

 63

Q: What sport did Joe DiMaggio play professionally: tennis, baseball or football?

A: Baseball

64

Q: What state is Las Vegas in?

A: Nevada

65

Q: Who sang that "you got to know when to hold 'em" and "know when to fold 'em"?

A: Kenny Rogers

66

Q: What country in North America uses money called the *peso*?

A: Mexico

Q: What country is famous for leprechauns and shamrocks?

A: Ireland

Q: Is TV's *Nickelodeon* named after a music machine, a money machine or a movie machine?

A: A music machine

Q: What do the initials SPF stand for?

A: Sun Protection Factor

70

Q: Where was Dorothy Hamill a winner: on the ice, in outer space or on a mountain?

A: On the ice

71

Q: What TV show gave Adam Sandler his big break?

A: *Saturday Night Live*

72

Q: What do you call tiny records with only one song on each side?

A: 45s

 Q: What song did a group called USA for Africa record in 1985?

A: "We Are the World"

 Q: What color are most sapphires?

A: Blue

 Q: In what language are most operas sung?

A: Italian

Q: What TV show featured a man named Mr. Green Jeans?

A: *Captain Kangaroo*

Q: What is the name of the first book of *The Bible*?

A: Genesis

Q: What country is known for chocolates and cuckoo clocks?

A: Switzerland

79

Q: Is Europe a peninsula, a continent or an island?

A: A continent

80

Q: What is Richard Simmons' usual outfit: a sharkskin suit, a robe and slippers or a tank top and shorts?

A: A tank top and shorts

81

Q: New York City has two major daily newspapers. Name one.

A: *The New York Times, The New York Post*

82

Q: What singer had hits like "Peggy Sue" and "That'll Be the Day" before he died in a 1959 plane crash?

A: Buddy Holly

83

Q: What math subject features the study of triangles?

A: Geometry

84

Q: What kind of illness is disco associated with: rash, fever or nausea?

A: Fever

Q: What band did Jerry Garcia perform with most?

A: The Grateful Dead

Q: What hairstyle, popular in the 1970s, also describes a bird part?

A: The feather cut

Q: Which author is known for her romance novels: Erma Bombeck, Danielle Steel or Beatrix Potter?

A: Danielle Steel

88

Q: What TV show featured the life of Laura Ingalls Wilder?

A: *Little House on the Prairie*

89

Q: What large South American country's capital is Rio de Janeiro: Bolivia, Chile or Brazil?

A: Brazil

90

Q: Dick is a common nickname for what first name?

A: Richard

Q: Name the Volkswagen Beetle turned racecar that was the star of several Disney movies.

A: Herbie (The Love Bug)

Q: Does a seismograph measure wind, rain or earthquakes?

A: Earthquakes

Q: When did the US celebrate its bicentennial (or 200th birthday)?

A: 1976

Q: Name at least two of the zany Marx Brothers.

A: Groucho, Harpo, Zeppo, Gummo, Chico

Q: What Illinois city is known as The Windy City?

A: Chicago

Q: Name at least four of the original 13 colonies.

A: Connecticut, Delaware, Georgia, Maryland, Massachusetts, New Hampshire, New Jersey, New York, North Carolina, Pennsylvania, Rhode Island, South Carolina, Virginia

Q: What state is famous for volcanoes, hula dancers and flower garlands called leis?

A: Hawaii

Q: What are the names of President John F. Kennedy's two children?

A: John, Jr. and Caroline

Q: Was *Love: American Style* a clothing company, a TV show or a best-selling novel?

A: A TV show

100

Q: Name the country that is very close to Florida and is led by a man with a beard named Fidel Castro.

A: Cuba

101

Q: What animal is used to make pork chops?

A: The pig

102

Q: What popular TV show starred comedienne Lucille Ball and her husband Desi Arnaz?

A: *I Love Lucy*

103

Q: What city, famous for a tea party, is called Beantown?

A: Boston

104

Q: Which of these was a popular video game in the 1980s: Bogus Battle, Space Invaders or GI Attack Zone?

A: Space Invaders

105

Q: Bono is the lead singer of what rock band?

A: U2

106

Q: The US once dropped atomic bombs on Hiroshima and Nagasaki. What country are these cities in?

A: Japan

107

Q: Mick Jagger and Keith Richards belong to what band?

A: The Rolling Stones

108

Q: What is the main ingredient in guacamole?

A: Avocado

109

Q: What swamp animal is on Izod shirts?

A: The alligator

110

Q: What famous scientist had a hard time in school but later came up with the theory of relativity?

A: Albert Einstein

111

Q: Was the TV show *The Waltons* about identical twins, a big family or newlyweds?

A: A big family

Q: The actor who gave Shrek his voice also plays Austin Powers. What's his name?

A: Mike Myers

Q: Porsches and BMWs are designed in what country?

A: Germany

Q: If you come across a crème brûlée, should you run from it, wear it or eat it?

A: Eat it (It's a delicious dessert!)

 Q: What comic strip did Charles Schulz create?

A: *Peanuts*

 Q: What is the most popular last name in the United States: Washington, Smith or Jones?

A: Smith

 Q: Manx cats are missing something. Is it a tail, their ears or hair?

A: A tail

Q: Who was President Ronald Reagan's vice president?

A: George Herbert Walker Bush

Q: What TV show starred Kermit the Frog and Miss Piggy, among others?

A: *The Muppet Show*

Q: Michael Jordan led what team to six NBA championships?

A: The Chicago Bulls

Q: Which of these kinds of poems did William Shakespeare write: haikus, limericks or sonnets?

A: Sonnets

Q: If it's noon in Seattle, what time is it in New York?

A: 3 p.m.

Q: What famous collie starred in movies and her own TV show?

A: Lassie

 124

Q: If you sang "The Day the Music Died," what would you sing after "Bye, bye, Miss American Pie"?

A: "Drove my Chevy to the levee but the levee was dry"

 125

Q: Mutton chops and cookie dusters are both kinds of what: men's facial hair, birds or eating utensils?

A: Men's facial hair

 126

Q: What country once had a buffalo nickel?

A: The United States

 127 Q: In Italy, what frozen treat is more common than ice cream?

A: Gelato

 128 Q: What Detroit record company introduced The Supremes, The Jackson 5 and more?

A: Motown

 129 Q: What is the name of the magic dragon that lived by the sea in a land called Honah Lee?

A: Puff

130

Q: What city has a giant clock named Big Ben and a bridge that a song says is falling down?

A: London

131

Q: What circus founder once said, "There's a sucker born every minute"?

A: P.T. Barnum

132

Q: What kind of animal was TV's Mr. Ed?

A: A horse, of course!

133

Q: Elephants are found on which two continents?

A: Asia and Africa

134

Q: What kind of jewel is it customary for a man to give a woman when he asks her to marry him?

A: A diamond

135

Q: What team did Mr. T belong to on a popular 1980s TV show?

A: *The A-Team*

136

Q: Firestone and Goodyear both are brands of what?

A: Tires

137

Q: If you referred to a Mr. Jones as "the late Mr. Jones," what are you saying about him?

A: That he is dead

138

Q: What 1970s remake of *The Wizard of Oz* starred Diana Ross and Michael Jackson?

A: *The Wiz*

 139

Q: What kind of music is Dolly Parton famous for singing: country, the blues or opera?

A: Country

 140

Q: What animal's hair is used to make wool sweaters?

A: Sheep

 141

Q: What really tall mountain did Sir Edmund Hillary first climb?

A: Mount Everest

Q: In what culture do 13-year-old kids celebrate bar mitzvahs (for boys) and bat mitzvahs (for girls)?

A: The Jewish culture

Q: Were The Mamas and The Papas a line of frozen dinners, a rock group or a series of kids' books?

A: A rock group

Q: If you take your coffee black, what do you add to it?

A: Nothing

145

Q: In what movie did an alien want to "phone home"?

A: *E.T.: The Extra-Terrestrial*

146

Q: What country did Winston Churchill once lead: England, Canada or the United States?

A: England

147

Q: Which of these things does not appear on a driver's license: height, occupation or eye color?

A: Occupation

Q: How many days are in the month of April?

A: 30

Q: Name two of the faces carved into Mount Rushmore.

A: George Washington, Thomas Jefferson, Abraham Lincoln, Teddy Roosevelt

Q: What musical instrument did Jimi Hendrix play: the piano, the harmonica or the guitar?

A: The guitar

 151

Q: Famed musicians Stevie Wonder and Ray Charles do not have the use of one of their senses. What is it?

A: Sight

 152

Q: What famous boxer claimed to "float like a butterfly" and "sting like a bee"?

A: Muhammad Ali

 153

Q: Where are Alcatraz, Angel and Treasure Islands?

A: In the San Francisco Bay

 154

Q: Which of these products blocks underarm sweat: antiperspirant or deodorant?

A: Antiperspirant

 155

Q: What sport did Joe Namath play professionally: football, basketball or hockey?

A: Football

 156

Q: A zoologist specializes in the study of what?

A: Animals

157

Q: Is Ray-Ban® a brand of skis, sunglasses or crystal?

A: Sunglasses

158

Q: What movie, set during the Civil War, tells the story of Scarlett O'Hara and Rhett Butler?

A: *Gone with the Wind*

159

Q: What system of measurement is used by virtually every country in the world, except the US?

A: The metric system

160

Q: You're traveling from California to Hawaii. What body of water will you cross?

A: The Pacific Ocean

161

Q: Who are Larry, Curly and Moe?

A: The Three Stooges

162

Q: Where would you use a Coleman® stove: in a school cafeteria, in your kitchen or at a campground?

A: At a campground

 163

Q: Which of these images is not seen when you look at the moon: a man's face, a bicycle or a rabbit?

A: A bicycle

 164

Q: What US President assured Americans that "I am not a crook" before he resigned in 1974?

A: Richard Nixon

 165

Q: Does Spike Lee make movies, soup or motorcycles?

A: Movies

166

Q: Name the band, led by a guy named Sting, that had hits like "De, Do Do Do, De Da Da Da."

A: The Police

167

Q: In the US, we call our local law enforcers police officers. What are they called in England?

A: Constables

168

Q: How many inches are in a foot?

A: 12

169

Q: Who painted the Mona Lisa: Claude Monet, Leonardo da Vinci or Diego Rivera?

A: Leonardo da Vinci

170

Q: Is Perrier a book, a sparkling water or a dog breed?

A: A sparkling water

171

Q: What movie starred John Belushi and Dan Aykroyd as brothers?

A: *The Blues Brothers*

Q: Who was the first person to fly alone across the Atlantic Ocean in an airplane?

A: Charles Lindbergh

Q: Who won the battle of the Alamo: the US or Mexico?

A: Mexico

Q: What TV show starring Alan Alda was broadcast for 11 years?

A: *M*A*S*H*

175

Q: What country would you visit to see a koala or a kangaroo?

A: Australia

176

Q: Please finish this Ray Parker, Jr. song's chorus:
   "Who ya gonna call?"

A: Ghostbusters!

177

Q: Meg, Peg and Marge are common nicknames for what
   first name?

A: Margaret

Q: Karl Marx described the principles behind what system of government: capitalism or communism?

A: Communism

Q: What singer/actress was once married to Sonny Bono and won an Academy Award® for *Moonstruck*?

A: Cher

Q: Is gingham a kind of cookie, fabric or rabbit?

A: Fabric

Q: Wasabi and pickled ginger are commonly served with what kind of food?

A: Sushi

Q: Which of the 50 states is named for a US president?

A: Washington

Q: Which one of these authors wrote *The Time Machine*: Stephen King, A.A. Milne or H.G. Wells?

A: H.G. Wells

184

Q: Name the four states that border Mexico.

A: California, Arizona, New Mexico and Texas

185

Q: Where does Casey Kasem do most of his work: on the radio, on TV or in books?

A: On the radio

186

Q: What do you call it when you pay someone to paint your toenails?

A: A pedicure

187

Q: Who was in movies like *Fatal Attraction* and *The Big Chill* before she played Cruella DeVille?

A: Glenn Close

188

Q: What kind of animals do you have if you run a dairy?

A: Cows

189

Q: Before remote controls were invented, how did people change the channel on their TVs?

A: They turned a dial.

 190

Q: What comedian used to wear an arrow through his head and say, "Well, excuuuuuuuuse me!"

A: Steve Martin

 191

Q: Which is not a hat: pillbox, fedora or sandwich?

A: Sandwich

 192

Q: If you're driving and see a police car with its lights flashing behind you, what should you do?

A: Pull over and stop

 193

Q: What two continents are in the Western Hemisphere?

A: North America and South America

 194

Q: Are stilettos high-heeled shoes, Italian cookies or opera singers?

A: High-heeled shoes

 195

Q: What kind of movies did Alfred Hitchcock make: thrillers, musicals or westerns?

A: Thrillers

196

Q: If you're allergic to peanuts, what should you not order in a Chinese restaurant: pot stickers, kung pao chicken or mu shu pork?

A: Kung pao chicken

197

Q: Where are Hershey® bars made?

A: Hershey, Pennsylvania

198

Q: Who was Paul Simon's funky singing partner until 1970?

A: Art Garfunkel

199

Q: What movies starred Peter Sellers as Inspector Clouseau and featured a cartoon at the beginning?

A: *The Pink Panther* movies

200

Q: Is orange pekoe a kind of peacock, tea or lipstick?

A: Tea

201

Q: Which US president once starred in movies with a monkey named Bonzo?

A: Ronald Reagan

202

Q: What TV show featured two CHP officers named Ponch and Jon?

A: *CHiPs*

203

Q: What religion follows the teachings of a prophet named Mohammed?

A: Islam (or the Muslim religion)

204

Q: Davy Crockett is known for wearing what kind of hat?

A: A coonskin cap

205

Q: What was *Romper Room*: a funhouse, a TV show for kids or a rock band?

A: A TV show for kids

206

Q: Which state is known as The Garden State?

A: New Jersey

207

Q: The word kindergarten means "children's garden" in what language?

A: German

Q: Was Esther Williams famous for sewing, swimming or swearing?

A: Swimming

Q: Which planet, known as the Red Planet, was once thought to be populated by little green men?

A: Mars

Q: What package delivery company uses brown trucks?

A: UPS

211

Q: Farrah Fawcett, Jaclyn Smith and Kate Jackson were the original stars of what '70s TV show?

A: *Charlie's Angels*

212

Q: If a clock's big hand is on the 4 and its little hand is on the 4, what time is it?

A: 4:20

213

Q: What language is spoken in Denmark?

A: Danish

214

Q: What war did the United States fight both to its east and to its west from 1941 to 1945?

A: World War II

215

Q: Who was Courtney Love married to?

A: Kurt Cobain (lead singer of Nirvana)

216

Q: What kind of airplane ticket gives you the biggest seats and the best food: coach, first class or stand-by?

A: First class

 Q: What part of speech is the word "she"?

A: A pronoun

 Q: What Georgia city houses the Coca-Cola headquarters and Dr. Martin Luther King's church?

A: Atlanta

 Q: Before he was The Joker in *Batman*, this actor starred in *One Flew Over the Cuckoo's Nest*. Who is he?

A: Jack Nicholson

Q: What TV show, named for a Texas city, featured a villain named J.R. Ewing?

A: *Dallas*

Q: What used to be where your belly button is?

A: Your umbilical cord

Q: What sport banned Tonya Harding?

A: Ice skating

223

Q: All essays must have an introduction. What other two components must they have?

A: A body and a conclusion

224

Q: What holiday is celebrated on All Saints Day eve?

A: Halloween

225

Q: What TV show featured a group of castaways, including the Skipper, the Professor and Ginger?

A: *Gilligan's Island*

Questions for Grown-Ups

Q: In what sport would you use a Nimbus 2000?

A: Quidditch

Q: Recite the pledge of allegiance.

A: "I pledge allegiance to the flag of the United States of America and to the Republic for which it stands, one Nation under God, indivisible, with liberty and justice for all."

Q: What is the first rank in the Boy Scouts?

A: Tenderfoot

Q: Who goes on adventures with a monkey named Boots?

A: Dora the Explorer

Q: Name two of the four Inner Planets (closest to the Sun).

A: Earth, Mars, Venus, Mercury

Q: Is a Mongoose a BMX bike, a kite or a surfboard?

A: A BMX bike

Q: Which month is Black History Month?

A: February

Q: In soccer, how many red cards can a player be given before being ejected from the game?

A: One

Q: In the movie *Monsters, Inc.*, what are the monsters trying to collect from the kids?

A: Screams

 Q: Which of these pop stars sings "Candy": Christina Aguilera, Mandy Moore or Britney Spears?

A: Mandy Moore

 Q: In which city does Madeline live?

A: Paris

 Q: Is Zoboo on *Zoboomafoo* a lemur, a spider monkey or a meerkat?

A: A lemur

 13

Q: What candy brand invites you to "taste the rainbow"?

A: Skittles

 14

Q: Which one of these books was written by Cynthia Rylant: *Missing May*, *Garfield* or *Sarah, Plain and Tall*?

A: *Missing May*

 15

Q: What California amusement park features Pirates of the Caribbean?

A: Disneyland

Q: What is Super Monkey Ball: a video game, a cartoon or a playground sport?

A: A video game

Q: Name the three ships that sailed with Christopher Columbus.

A: Nina, Pinta, Santa Maria

Q: What kind of animal is Clifford?

A: A big red dog

Q: Name the two girls who hang out with Scooby-Doo.

A: Daphne and Velma

Q: Which dinosaur is bigger: Tyrannosaurus Rex, Mussaurus or Brachiosaurus?

A: Brachiosaurus

Q: Which ocean is the biggest: Pacific, Indian, Atlantic or Arctic?

A: Pacific

Q: What are the names of the three Powerpuff Girls?

A: Bubbles, Buttercup and Blossom

Q: What is the last line of the poem "'Twas the Night Before Christmas"?

A: "Merry Christmas to all and to all a good night!"

Q: What is the child holding on the cover of the Andrew Clement's book *The Janitor's Boy*: a broom, a key or a trash can?

A: A key

 Q: What pop group sings the song "Bye Bye Bye"?

A: *NSYNC

 Q: How many continents are there on Earth?

A: 7

 Q: What explorer gave a fantastic description of Asia: Columbus, Vasco de Gama or Marco Polo?

A: Marco Polo

Q: What song features the phrase "heigh-ho the dairy-o"?

A: "The Farmer in the Dell"

Q: What grade are kids usually in when they start high school?

A: Ninth

Q: Mrs. Birkbeck's fourth grade class is in the state of Georgia. What is the capital of Georgia?

A: Atlanta

Q: Where does SpongeBob SquarePants work: The Rusty Pelican, The Krusty Krab or The Fussy Skipper?

A: The Krusty Krab

Q: Who wrote *Little Women*?

A: Louisa May Alcott

Q: What's the longest river in the world: the Nile, the Amazon or the Yang Tze?

A: The Nile

Q: What is the first name of the lead character in *Lord of the Rings: The Fellowship of the Ring?*

A: Frodo (Baggins)

Q: Which of these states is not on the Chesapeake Bay: Delaware, Virginia, Rhode Island or Maryland?

A: Rhode Island

Q: What color are Barney's spots?

A: Green

Q: What is the name of the Pokemon main character that is large and yellow?

A: Pikachu

Q: How do you spell Britney Spears' first name?

A: B-R-I-T-N-E-Y

Q: Name at least three of the four girls who sing the remake of the song "Lady Marmalade."

A: Pink, Maya, Li'l Kim, Christina Aguilera

Q: How many feet are in a mile: 3,280, 5,280, or 6,280?

A: 5,280

Q: What song includes the line "land of the Pilgrim's pride": "God Bless America," "My Country 'Tis of Thee" or "America the Beautiful"?

A: "My Country 'Tis of Thee"

Q: In *The Simpsons*, who is Milhouse's best friend?

A: Bart

43

Q: Harry Potter has two best friends, a boy and a girl. What is the boy's name?

A: Ron Weasley

44

Q: What is the answer to a division problem called?

A: Quotient

45

Q: Who was the King of England during the American Revolution?

A: King George III

Q: Who won the 2001 World Series?

A: The Arizona Diamondbacks

Q: What kind of dinosaur is the star of the movie *Jurassic Park III*?

A: Spinosaurus

Q: Who wrote *Tales of a Fourth Grade Nothing*?

A: Judy Blume

Q: Is George W. Bush the 36th, 43rd or 51st President of the United States?

A: 43rd

Q: Was the Xbox created by Sony, Nintendo, Microsoft or Sega?

A: Microsoft

Q: What colorful nickname was given to English soldiers during The Revolutionary War?

A: Redcoats

Q: In the comic *Calvin and Hobbes*, what kind of animal is Hobbes?

A: Tiger

Q: What is Justin Timberlake's favorite color?

A: Baby blue

Q: Name the four presidents on Mt. Rushmore.

A: George Washington, Abraham Lincoln, Theodore Roosevelt, Thomas Jefferson

Q: On the TV series *Courage the Cowardly Dog*, what is Courage afraid of?

A: Monsters

Q: What scared Little Miss Muffett?

A: A spider

Q: What is Homer Simpson's favorite food?

A: Donuts

Q: Name the runaway slave who was killed in the Boston Massacre: Dred Scott, Crispus Attucks or Benjamin Adams.

A: Crispus Attucks

Q: What are the four food groups?

A: Meat/fish, dairy, grains and fruits/vegetables

Q: Name the player who, at 15, was the youngest person to ever play for the US Women's National Soccer Team.

A: Mia Hamm

 61

Q: Which is not a marsupial: kangaroo, possum or panda bear?

A: Panda bear

62

Q: Which band is Nick Carter in?

A: The Backstreet Boys

 63

Q: How many stars are on the American flag?

A: 50

64

Q: Who is not a skateboarder: Mark Gonzalez, Poncho Moler or Dave Mirra?

A: Dave Mirra

65

Q: What colors are the Cartoon Network's logo?

A: Black and white

66

Q: The answer to a multiplication problem is called a what?

A: Product

Q: Where does the Muffin Man live?

A: Down on Drury Lane

Q: What is the last name of *NSYNC's Lance: Fatone, Bass or Wahlberg?

A: Bass

Q: What brand of gum has a flame over the letter "i" on its packaging?

A: Big Red

Q: In *Captain Underpants*, what is George's last name?

A: Beard

Q: What are the three steps a person should take if they're on fire?

A: Stop, drop and roll

Q: What is the small Oreo® cookie called: Tiny-Oreo, Mini-Oreo or Baby-Oreo?

A: Mini-Oreo®

Q: Name one of the three periods in the Mesozoic Era, when dinosaurs lived.

A: Triassic, Jurassic, Cretaceous

Q: What is the name of the cat on *Sabrina, the Teenage Witch*?

A: Salem

Q: What is Tommy Pickle's baby brother's name?

A: Dylan (Dil)

Q: What did Tom, Tom the Piper's son steal?

A: A pig

Q: Find the pronoun in this sentence: She ate green soup.

A: She

Q: What kid detective has a first name that is a kind of book and a last name that is a color?

A: Encyclopedia Brown

79

Q: What type of nuclear reaction splits a heavy atomic nucleus into two lighter ones?

A: Fission

80

Q: What is the name of the stuffed animal that a boy named Chester suspects is a vampire?

A: Bunnicula

81

Q: What is the nickname of the state of Texas?

A: The Lonestar State

Q: In what country is the Suez Canal located?

A: Egypt

Q: Which of these is not a real comic book character: Elektra, Dredd Head or Hellboy?

A: Dredd Head

Q: Does Vanessa Carlton sing songs or star in a TV show?

A: She sings songs

85

Q: Is Roxy a brand of clothes, a teen magazine or a pop star?

A: A brand of clothes

86

Q: On the cartoon *Rugrats*, what is Tommy's last name?

A: Pickles

87

Q: Simplify the fraction 42/6.

A: 7

88

Q: What is the name of Big Bird's hairy, brown friend—the one that everyone thought was imaginary?

A: Mr. Snuffleupagus

89

Q: What badger book character loves bread and jam?

A: Frances

90

Q: What is the name of the headmaster at Hogwarts School of Witchcraft and Wizardry?

A: Albus Dumbledore

 91

Q: True or false: lines of latitude are also called meridians.

A: False (they are called parallels)

 92

Q: Name Blue's pink dog friend on *Blue's Clues*.

A: Magenta

 93

Q: Who wrote *The Boy Who Cried Wolf*: The Brothers Grimm, Aesop or Uncle Remus?

A: Aesop

Q: In the movie *Shrek*, what is the name of the princess Shrek is trying to save?

A: Princess Fiona

Q: On which network can *Dexter's Laboratory* be found?

A: Cartoon Network

Q: Is Cape Horn located at the southern tip of South America or the southern tip of Africa?

A: The southern tip of South America

97

Q: What type of animal is Arthur?

A: An aardvark

98

Q: What is the Smucker's product that puts peanut butter and jelly together in one jar?

A: Goober

99

Q: What does the online abbreviation BBL stand for?

A: Be Back Later

Q: The oldest surviving college in North America was founded in 1636. Was it Harvard, Stanford or Yale?

A: Harvard

Q: On the cartoon *Rugrats*, what is the name of Angelica's cat?

A: Fluffy

Q: Is the word "quickly" an adjective or an adverb?

A: An adverb

Q: Name the wild redhead with a pet monkey named Mr. Nilsson.

A: Pippi Longstocking

Q: Which state has the most congressional representatives: Texas, California or neither?

A: California

Q: What rock band sings the 2001 song "In the End"?

A: Linkin Park

 106

Q: Name the sarcastic teenager from Lawndale who has her own TV show.

A: Daria

 107

Q: What are the four factors of the number 15?

A: 1, 3, 5, 15

 108

Q: *The Bad Beginning* and *The Hostile Hospital* are both part of what book series?

A: *A Series of Unfortunate Events*

109

Q: What substance in green plants turns water and carbon dioxide into sugars that help the plant grow?

A: Chlorophyll

110

Q: Which of these is not a skateboarding company: Flip, Armpit or Spitfire?

A: Armpit

111

Q: Who released the album *Country Grammar* in 2000?

A: Nelly

Q: Which rap artist made the album *Word of Mouf*?

A: Ludacris

Q: Alaina's grandfather is 76 years old. Her grandmother is an octogenarian. Which grandparent is older?

A: Her grandmother (Octogenarians are in their 80s.)

Q: At which of these places can you find people spelunking: a cave, an airport or an oil well?

A: A cave

 Q: Which of these angles is equal to 90 degrees: a right angle, an obtuse angle or an acute angle?

A: A right angle

 Q: What popular story features characters named Fern and Wilbur?

A: *Charlotte's Web*

 Q: Who is the lead singer in the band No Doubt?

A: Gwen Stefani

Q: When did the Wright Brothers make the first manned plane flight: 1903, 1913 or 1933?

A: 1903

Q: What band sings "Give Me Just One Night (Una Noche)"?

A: 98°

Q: What country sold Alaska to the US in 1867?

A: Russia

Q: What grade is Bart Simpson in: fourth, fifth or sixth?

A: Fourth

Q: If Steve is playing right-handed tennis and a ball bounces to his left, should he hit a forehand or a backhand?

A: Backhand

Q: The *Animaniacs* are siblings. What is the sister's name?

A: Dot

Q: Who is SpongeBob SquarePants' boss?

A: Mr. Krabs

Q: Macaulay Culkin starred as what character in the movie *Home Alone*: Eric, Brian or Kevin?

A: Kevin

Q: What kind of animal is Anna Sewell's *Black Beauty*?

A: A horse

Q: Which of these words refers to a group of islands: isthmus, peninsula or archipelago?

A: Archipelago

Q: What is the square root of 144?

A: 12

Q: Does Beverly Cleary's Ramona have an older sister named Beverly, Beezus or Bathsheeba?

A: Beezus

130

Q: How are Brian and Kevin of The Backstreet Boys related?

A: They are cousins.

131

Q: Is Master P's first name Percy, Paul or Poindexter?

A: Percy

132

Q: What is the correct spelling of the word "strait" when it means a narrow channel of water?

A: S-T-R-A-I-T

Q: How many turtles go into one quart of mock turtle soup?

A: None

Q: Do the seeds of a flower grow in the stamen, the petals or the pistil?

A: The pistil

Q: What Disney movie, made in 2000, features Mandy Moore, Anne Hathaway and Julie Andrews?

A: *The Princess Diaries*

Q: What two adjectives describe the kind of soul
Old King Cole was?

A: Merry, old

Q: Who created the game Super Smash Brothers: Blizzard
Entertainment or Hal Laboratories?

A: Hal Laboratories

Q: Which is two words: haystack, hay fever or haywire?

A: Hay fever

 139

Q: In what movie did Britney Spears make her motion picture debut?

A: *Crossroads*

 140

Q: What language does Dora the Explorer speak besides English?

A: Spanish

 141

Q: Is "Jumpin' Jumpin'" sung by Vitamin C, Outkast or Destiny's Child?

A: Destiny's Child

Q: What is the decimal for five hundredths?

A: .05

Q: What is the name of Limp Bizkit's lead singer: Fred Durst, Flea or Kid Rock?

A: Fred Durst

Q: Which of these marine animals is not an invertebrate: a lobster, a seal or a squid?

A: A seal

145

Q: On Instant Messenger, what does TTYL stand for?

A: Talk To You Later

146

Q: Who built Machu Picchu, the lost city in the Andes Mountains of Peru: the Mayans or the Incas?

A: The Incan Civilization (The Incas)

147

Q: What does Johnny Bravo try to get in every episode of his cartoon show: food, a car or a girlfriend?

A: A girlfriend

Q: What restaurant makes the Mighty Kids Meal?

A: McDonald's

Q: What do you call a 7-sided polygon?

A: Heptagon

Q: In Disney's *Beauty and the Beast*, what animal does the footstool become when the spell is broken?

A: A dog

Q: Is Tony Hawk a skateboarder, a surfer or a soccer player?

A: Skateboarder

Q: The term "zoinks" is used in what popular cartoon?

A: *Scooby-Doo*

Q: In Henry Wadsworth Longfellow's poem about a little girl, where is her little curl?

A: Right in the middle of her forehead

154

Q: What do you call a triangle that has three equal sides and three equal angles?

A: Equilateral triangle

155

Q: Where do the Powerpuff Girls® live: Happy Valley, Metrozone or Townsville?

A: Townsville

156

Q: How do you write 2,561 in expanded notation?

A: 2,000 + 500 + 60 + 1

 Q: What is the three little kittens' reward for finding their mittens?

A: Pie

 Q: Is a long, unbroken series of waves called a trough, a crest, or a swell?

A: A swell

 Q: What is the name of Barney's big, yellow friend?

A: BJ

160

Q: Name the boys who live next door to Bart Simpson.

A: Rod and Todd Flanders

161

Q: What are the first six words of Abraham Lincoln's Gettysburg Address?

A: "Four score and seven years ago"

162

Q: What sisters moved out of a *Full House* and now have their own clothing line?

A: Mary-Kate and Ashley Olsen

 163

Q: The career of the musical group O-Town was documented on which TV show?

A: *Making the Band*

 164

Q: What is the center of the earth called?

A: The core

 165

Q: The McTwist and the Caballerial are tricks named after two athletes in what sport?

A: Skateboarding

Q: What is the first name of Sugar Ray's lead singer: Mike, Marv or Mark?

A: Mark

Q: What state's capital is named for the 16th President of the US?

A: Nebraska (Lincoln)

Q: What does BMX stand for?

A: Bicycle Motocross

169

Q: Which of these tiny particles has one unit of positive electricity: an electron, a neutron or a proton?

A: A proton

170

Q: Which cereal company makes Lucky Charms?

A: General Mills

171

Q: What actress plays a teenage witch and runs Hartbreak Films with her mom?

A: Melissa Joan Hart

 172

Q: What does Usher's album *8701* stand for?

A: The album's release date (August 7, 2001)

 173

Q: What does Alanna in the *Alanna* book series want to be: a star, a princess or a warrior?

A: A warrior

 174

Q: Which *Dawson's Creek* character does Kerr Smith play: Dawson, Joey or Jack?

A: Jack

Q: What 2001 animated film features a preteen genius?

A: *Jimmy Neutron: Boy Genius*

Q: In a fraction, what do you call the number that shows how many equal parts the whole has been divided into?

A: Denominator

Q: What did the Little Engine that Could like to say?

A: I think I can, I think I can.

Q: What actress debuted as Olivia Kendall in *The Cosby Show* and went on to star as Charisse in *Dr. Dolittle*?

A: Raven-Symone

Q: Name all four of the Earth's oceans.

A: Atlantic, Pacific, Indian and Arctic

Q: In soccer, what color is the warning card that is given for repeated fouls or abusive language?

A: Yellow

181

Q: What does the G rating of a movie stand for?

A: General Audiences

182

Q: What story features a nice couple named Jim Dear and Darling?

A: *Lady and the Tramp*

183

Q: Name the sentence that introduces the main idea of a paragraph.

A: Topic sentence

Q: What do you call a four-sided shape whose opposite sides are parallel and equal?

A: Parallelogram

Q: What lil' six-year-old made his recording debut on Snoop Doggy Dogg's 1993 album?

A: Lil' Bow Wow

Q: Name Peter Rabbit's three sisters.

A: Flopsy, Mopsy and Cotton-tail

Q: If you "puff" your shoes, what are you doing?

A: Putting an extra sock under the tongue to make the shoe look bigger

---

Q: Who took Steve's place on *Blue's Clues*?

A: His brother, Joe

Q: Ray wants to buy a $20 video game. He has $20.50, and sales tax is 8%. Does he have enough money?

A: No (the total is $21.60 with tax)

 190

Q: In science experiments, what is the element called that changes with each trial?

A: Dependent variable

 191

Q: Name the storybook bull who prefers smelling flowers to fighting.

A: Ferdinand

 192

Q: What Alaskan mountain has the highest peak in North America?

A: Denali (Mount McKinley)

Q: Name the first movie based on *The Lord of the Rings* book trilogy.

A: *The Fellowship of the Ring*

Q: What do you call an angle that is less than 90 degrees?

A: Acute

Q: Is David Lascher on *That '70s Show*, *Sabrina the Teenage Witch* or *Friends*?

A: *Sabrina the Teenage Witch*

Q: Is Dr. Seuss' Horton (of *Horton Hears a Who*) an elephant, a mongoose or a giraffe?

A: An elephant

Q: Who was the first American woman since Peggy Fleming to win three world titles in figure skating?

A: Michelle Kwan

Q: In the movie *Shrek*, what is the name of the donkey?

A: Donkey

199

Q: What do the 13 stripes on the US flag represent?

A: The original 13 colonies

200

Q: What real life couple was chosen to play Fred and Daphne in 2002's *Scooby-Doo*?

A: Freddie Prinze Jr. and Sarah Michelle Gellar

201

Q: Who created the Conker Games: Rareware, UN Talk or Neversoft?

A: Rareware

Q: With whom did the Gingham Dog get in a tussle?

A: The Calico Cat

Q: Name the member of the Funnie family who has his own show on the Disney Channel.

A: Doug

Q: What is the literary term for a description that gives an object human qualities?

A: Personification

205

Q: Which Dr. Seuss story features Thing One and Thing Two?

A: *The Cat in the Hat*

206

Q: Singer Alicia Moore, who likes to "Get the Party Started," has what colorful stage name?

A: Pink

207

Q: The Gobi Desert is located on what continent?

A: Asia

208

Q: What sport features flatlanding: BMX riding, snowshoeing or surfing?

A: BMX riding

209

Q: In Disney's *Beauty and the Beast*, what is the name of the character that is a candle?

A: Lumiere

210

Q: Who is Jessica Simpson married to?

A: Nick Lachay

211

Q: What shape is the scar on Harry Potter's forehead?

A: Lightning Bolt

212

Q: Mark swims the 800-yard freestyle. In a 25-yard pool, how many lengths of the pool will it take him to swim 800 yards?

A: 32

213

Q: What TV show co-stars Danielle Fishel as Topanga?

A: *Boy Meets World*

Q: Name the singer who appeared with Ashanti in his "Always on Time" music video.

A: Ja Rule

Q: In Mrs. Cristofani's class, 6 of the 30 students are girls. What percentage of the class is girls?

A: 20%

Q: In an online chat, what does ROTFL stand for?

A: Rolling on the Floor Laughing

Q: What book features a character named Meg Murray: *Matilda*, *A Wrinkle in Time* or *The Secret Garden*?

A: *A Wrinkle in Time*

Q: Which is farther north: Portland, Maine or Portland, Oregon?

A: Portland, Oregon

Q: What reality show gave Eden's Crush their start?

A: *Popstars*

220

Q: What part of speech is the word "colorful"?

A: Adjective

221

Q: In Mark Twain's *The Adventures of Tom Sawyer*, what is the name of Tom's girlfriend?

A: Becky Thatcher

222

Q: Is Dr. Dre's real name Andre Young or Desmond Raye?

A: Andre Young

 223

Q: Name three of the five states that border Illinois.

A: Wisconsin, Iowa, Missouri, Kentucky, Indiana

 224

Q: What kind of warrior is The Cartoon Network's Jack: a knight, a samurai or a boxer?

A: Samurai

 225

Q: What does ROYGBIV stand for?

A: Red, Orange, Yellow, Green, Blue, Indigo, Violet (the colors of the rainbow)

ABOUT THE AUTHOR

Bob Moog, co-founder of University Games and publisher of Spinner Books, has been creating games and puzzles and the like since childhood. He tormented his four younger siblings with quizzes, conundrums and physical and mental challenges during the 1960s. Now, he introduces the Spinner Books for Kids™ series, hoping it will challenge and puzzle you as much as his early "work" did his family 40 years ago.

Moog is the author of several other puzzle/game and children's books, including *Gummy Bear Goes to Camp*, *Kids Battle the Grown-Ups*™, *30 Second Mysteries*™ and *Secret Identities*™.